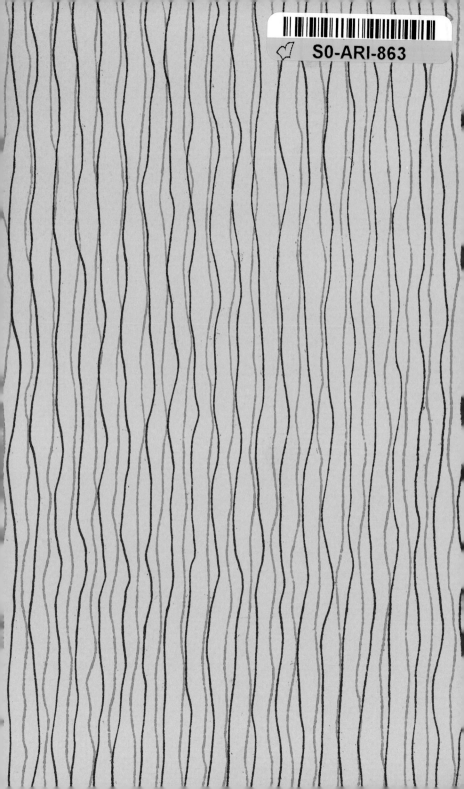

RATTLESNAKE GRASS

selected shorter poems
1956-1976

John Oliver Simon

Hanging Loose Press 1978

published by Hanging Loose Press
231 Wyckoff St.
Brooklyn, N.Y. 11217

Art by Harley Elliot

Some of these poems appeared in these journals & anthologies: *Aldebaran Review, Big River News, Califia, California Bicentennial Poets Anthology, Campfires of the Resistance, City of Buds & Flowers, Contemporaries, East Bay Review, Hanging Loose, In Youth, Kuksu, The Living Underground, Manroot, man.u.code, New American & Canadian Poetry, Only Humans With Songs to Sing, Open Education Exchange, The Pagan Trine, Poems read in the spirit of Peace & Gladness, Poetry Now, Praire Schooner, The Putney Magazine, Scree, Velvet Wings, Wormwood Review and Zahir.*

and in the following chapbooks:
    ROADS TO DAWN LAKE (Oyez, 1968)
    ADVENTURES OF THE FLOATING RABBI (Runcible Spoon, 1968)
    CAT POME (Gunrunner Press, 1969)
    THE WOODCHUCK WHO LIVES ON TOP OF MOUNT RITTER
    (Galactic Approximation, 1970)
    ANIMAL (Galactic Approximation, 1973)
    SNAKE'S TOOTH (Aldebaran Review, 1974)
    LIVING IN THE BONEYARD (Cat's Pajamas, 1975)

Hanging Loose Press wishes to thank the National Endowment for the Arts for the grant in support of this project.

Library of Congress Cataloging in Publication Data.

Simon, John Oliver.
Rattlesnake Grass.
I. Title.
PS3569.I4818R3   811'.5'4   78-52922
ISBN 0-914610-12-0

this book is for Jan

INTRODUCTION

It's a pleasure to introduce this selection of work by John Oliver Simon. In a day, for better or worse, when we often limit and locate poets as New Yorkers, New Englanders, Latin Americans and so on, John is clearly a Western poet. An early refugee from the East, California is his home. I almost said Berkeley. But that's not true. He lives in Berkeley. But his world is just as much informed by what has come to live through him from the Coastal ranges, the Sierras, and the deserts of this State. At 35 he has become a unique and clear part of a Western tradition of writing that comes down to us from Joaquin Miller, John Muir, Kenneth Rexroth and a strong host of other writers who have sought their own survival, and perhaps the survival of the whole race in what they have discovered in the Western landscape.

What gives John's work its special stamp and character is the new terms with which he has sought to clarify and define that survival. Unlike many of his elders, who were City-phobes at heart, *Rattlesnake Grass* reveals the evolution of a consciousness that has finally worked to unify what is found *outback* with the urban, the City life. What is exciting here is to watch how this path emerges over the years to take a resolved tone and shape. Like his elders, it is a path that starts perfectly willing and happy to stay out on a mountain of possible harmonies. Early on we get that mysterious and healing sense of excitement that comes from finding a voice and sense of total integration with a natural world:

> ...mysterious glyphic signs almost
> letters I make up to make up for my
> lack of learning
>
> one waterdrop reflecting sky &
> dank black ledges up above
> rich moss, star tendrill'd, hanging on

the shape I want to have in the air
the mistake that I was meant to
control the planet...

(from "A SINGLE LIVEOAK BRANCH, SECRET PATH")

What he experiences is an ecstatically felt, almost religious sense of conversion. Through intense struggle and concentration he finds he can become *at one* with the beauty and risk of a natural order. You can hear his sense of conviction in the righteous, but wonderful anger at the intruders, the colonials, the Sierra Clubbers in "THE WOODCHUCK WHO LIVES ON TOP OF MOUNT RITTER." Or in the "at home" comedy and bliss of "BLUEJAY MEDICINE EVENT," one of my favorite poems in the book.

But what is significant to John's work is the realization that "the mountain" is only one member of a larger partnership. He is not a nihilist in the mythical sense of Robinson Jeffers. The ultimate test of the consciousness here is whether or not it can survive the City. What is important is how the value of the mountain can be brought into what might be called "the urban wound." The desire for unification is paramount. It's here that we find the real dynamic and force behind John's growth as a poet and the significance of this volume.

The initial poems of The City phase bring us the troubling depth of the split. There is an almost untenable moving back and forth between what is found *pure*, an enchantment with what is found naturally resonant, and a voice of despair at what appears to be an unrecoverable death bent cosmos. The sense of mystery and pleasure in the "CAT POME" is broken by the unbalancing amazement in "this black guy comes out of my backyard at 1 AM." The hope and failure of People's Park permeates this section like a constant reminder. And the journeys out of the country, to Mexico ("BORDER"), and the Middle East ("GULHANE HOTEL POEM"), as if to escape what he has found in the City, again become means of illuminating what was presumed "natural" and is found torn by the intrusions of Europe and America.

But it is at this point of almost total disillusion without any prospects that this book turns, begins to resolve itself, and give wonderful reason for this occasion. A balance begins to occur. The experience, the knowledge of the wilderness begins to feed a vision of the City. The consciousness of both worlds unifies across an immediate field of perception. It happens most beautifully in "SPIRAL" where the natural shapes of the mountain afford a way into the domestic shapes of a City day. It starts out:

> kitchen match struck from sandstone of a
> half-glazed mug
> the most impossible detail
> spiral of bighorn sheep's one horn

and then literally spirals through house, landscape, memory, the present, until what is "territorial damage" winds into a simultaneously disparate and unified texture that just plain pleases as it occurs. And then, so that we are not totally overtaken by the radiance of "SPIRAL," he offers the flip side, the comic object of himself taking flight and song out of the Berkeley tideflats:

> I was flying over their heads,
> dragging tires, dripping mud in their faces

> (from "I came down to the stones of the bay")

What I think you will find in John Oliver Simon's work is a person who has taken the real risk of integrating those still available "natural knowledges" of self and landscape with what has become our technological inscape, our racial and sexual malaise. It is the major collision of our time. His willingness to meet it is a gift. The poems shift and shake, risk and retreat, and then move forward in the vibrancy of struggling to emerge. These poems are the gifts of the middle passage.

Stephen Vincent
San Francisco
December 27, 1977

The woodchuck who lives on top of Ritter is naturally a marmot. Same genus, *Marmota*. I didn't know. Similarly, in "A SINGLE LIVEOAK BRANCH," the seed of "chaparral broom" was probably of Coyote brush, *Baccharis sp.* The restaurant in "so many faces" was the Darvish; in recent years, however, they have been very supportive of street poets & deserve your patronage should you be on Telegraph Avenue.

J.O.S.

CONTENTS

I
1956-1964

LUNATIC NIGHT

Lunatic night, the moon pale silver
And the earth below a moon-lit skeleton,
Carved white marble, shaken by starwinds.
Nocturnal things, flecked with silver, hurrying,
Moving under the pale god of the night,
Pale god as dead as the cold stars.
Eye of the night, gazing
With a cold brilliance at
The horde of scurrying ghost-things
Vampires of the blood of the day earth,
Now gnawing the bones of the night earth,
Clean earth now touched with the rotten feet
Of decayed light.

Coming the dawn, as awakening from a nightmare,
Coming the orange sun, and the end of sleep,
Passing the moon, a pale small flag, out of the west,
And the cold ghost horde flees,
Back to their homes in the minds of men.

1956

I would be translucent,
bearing light through me like water,
like the laboring white sky
of an August morning.

I would be dark too,
wise, warm as the stone eyes
of some sunburnt Egyptian god
long, deep in the red shadows
of an August dusk.

1958

no flowers left in the fields
to tempt my imagination
into small things: the busyness
of gold and sapphire insects,
perfect stones, rich boxes
of melodious wood;
my eyes have grown.
Over the brown and barren fields
there is the wild air, and distance
as dumb as understanding.
I stop,
drown in examination.

1959

Self-knowledge is cold to the skin;
my love looks inward, only probing me,
(though if I love a beauty it is yours)
I live for you, but only love for me.

My failure is that I cannot be sky,
but all my joy is earthly, in the water's fall.
I stand between them, walking on earth,
noting my shadow's length,
my sound of voice,
loving the mirror's lie.

I should not pity me, that I am wasting
my time and love in pity, not in love;
for shadows mingle with the falling night,
and voices silence;
when mirrors break, the image is no more.
Give me to dance on earth, in love's illusion,
not self-regarding, but regarding you:
let me seek sunlight through the praising water
and not my own reflection;
                                    once, long since,
a boy forsook the sunlight for his image;
they say that where he knelt a flower grew.

1960

ENTANGLING

Once these words had been
given, my breath
into her hands, there was
a space, a moment, as when
tasting spoiled fruit, teeth
buried in the ripe
entangling,
a hesitation: suddenly
too far gone not to taste
the flavor in it, she
knew me. My hands
on hers, I had spoken
to her, the words
were gone. I had become
a naked man, animal
in all functions. Goat-beard
and the dripping mouth.

Flies clatter in the burst
mouth of the fruit, stone
beneath the skin, the sun
infests the burning flesh.

Afterwards, we had
fallen together.
I was not flattered.
I wanted a way of saying
to cast it out.

1963

II

The Mountain

GREEN APPLE BOOKS &
MUSIC PRESENTS
AN IN STORE APPEARANCE
CYRIL
JORDAN
OF THE FLAMING GROOVIES
FREE MUSIC AND ART SHOW
WITH SPECIAL GUESTS
MAY 23, 1999

4:00 PM

GREEN APPLE BOOKS
520 CLEMENT ST.
AT
SIXTH AVE.

SHAKE
SOME
ACTION

SUPERSTITION CANYON

the stone narrows to a dark door.
here, in seventy-nine,
they chased the Paiutes.
the troopers found no Indians.
Maybe once the air sprung
with an arrow, then with
stillness. There, one rock standing
like a dumb tooth. And the dark
drum of the sky.
                  or with clumsy
boots they started a snake from under
clattering rocks. Moving out of darkness.
in the canyon I learn to
move in this silence, with furtive hands
pressed against stone, as slow
as sun moves on the rim of sky.
the Indians took to the mountains.
they learned to live in the snow.
in the canyon, left their sentinels:
hammered on a dark rock, the sun's face,
the white eye and dancing hair.

DECEMBER 25

I heard no sheperds singing
between the mountain and the sea
slept under pine branches

christmas morning
jacked off thinking about you

stars glowing under mountain

I could sleep close to your
body. and be no closer

get up you fucking sun

THE WOODCHUCK WHO LIVES ON TOP OF MOUNT RITTER

the woodchuck who lives on top of Mount Ritter
don't take shit from nobody
you might see the golden
brown of him lying close down on the black
talus. you might see him scamp across the rocks

he lives on raisins, bread, sardines, chocolate
climbers leave — 7 parties made the top for instance
sunday 19 july 1970. every now and then
a gaggle of sierra clubbers with brand new ice axes
maybe 45 of them. this means a feast. weekdays
he might get some grubs, airborne spores
of trout — trout must have airborne spores
or they wouldn't be in Nydiver Lake
above Shadow Falls. who knows, weekdays
maybe he works the camps on Lake Ediza
but how does he get up & down the glacier.

the woodchuck, I think he is a woodchuck.
he lies in air & is cautious.
13 thousand feet of air
black rocks color of electricity
his throat is flattened against the
stone, watching me
dark eyes as those of us who came from water

his fur
on his front haunches rises & ripples
soft as yellow grass in the late
wind. his back same golden under
hair-backs brown as earth. now he's
eaten the bit of bread I
threw him. nostrils
gray quivering
if he cares he can
see Mt. Goddard, the Clark Range, hazy golden
rock and torn with snow beneath thunderheads.
ah woodchuck

does he have a wife, is he raising babies
to follow his trade — next summer, my child
the summit of Banner Peak will be yours.
when it thunders he waits
gently in talus caverns
far from danger. possibly with their soft bodies
leaning around him

the man who sees him goes downhill from this
phantasmic beast among incredible
colors, white snowbell cassiope, indian
paintbrush red with yellow spikes, the
purple and yellow he has no names, his
hands the earth the clouds the air the evening
star a black mountain
shoulder rising to catch it
his face does not see all the colors

the woodchuck who lives on top of Mount Ritter
is very careful and shows himself
only to those who come quiet and
with no intention to harm.
somebody has to
do what he is doing
because the waste from human
people must be consumed & changed into
gravity meadow grass stars insects & baby woodchucks.
I didn't write this in the summit register
for fear somebody would come from
Washington to check the woodchuck's headlights
and make him pay his income tax.
or rip off his mountain in the timehonored
tradition of what they are trying
to do to the universe

the night I went up to the top
of the world I met a king
on a gray throne tower
of a stone
kiln in the moonlight at the
top of the world

I met the king & he was me.

I said what
is my name. he
shook himself with a moon colored laughter & said
boy
what is the name of that mountain

BLUEJAY MEDICINE EVENT

a woman   gives a man a bluejay feather.
reflecting blue & barred across three times with black
he will wear it in his gray hat.

her contact lens   flips from her fingers somewhere thru
windy sun. they are on their knees
looking, their faces turned to the ground, pushing
chips of sugar pine bark aside with slow fingers, needles, grass,
cone scales, dry wood, scraps of granite, gray & warm brown
bark tumbling over & over underneath

they have been looking for two hours. fuck it, she screams
it's hopeless, why am I so stupid, I wish
I were dead. she goes crying half-blind to tend the fire

he has sectioned an area six or eight feet on a
side along the vector of wind. in the hurt he
begins to pray. bluejay help me find it
bluejay help me find it

he takes the jay feather & lets it flutter & searches
near the place where it lands without
success. she comes over dryeyed & bitter, tells him
you don't have to look anymore.
he says, I don't want to hear that.

he promises bread & popcorn to bluejay if he will help.
he takes the blue feather again & gives it
to the wind. it sticks in the brown needles
pointing upright. he approaches it slowly. where the
gray quill pricks down between pine fragments
the thin circle of plastic sitting on its edge hidden.

from the fire she hears a jaybird talking
in the high branches.

I shook my grandfather's hand.
"Well, I'll see you in the other world," he said.

I nodded.
"Yes, on the mountains in the other world."

My grandfather shook his head very slowly.
"There are no mountains in the other world," he said.

in Swarthmore College ethics class in 1961 we solemnly
      decided to shoot George Jackson
 rather than the piano player
  in case the planet was running out of food.

now who's got the intelligence to take the last bite:
    B-52 pilots trailing chemical ice
   towards the sundown mountains
      in a crooked sign of glory
or Jan & me tired & sunburned by the stone
   of the fire in the wash
     with our nylon & sulphur technology
  or Cin Que whispering into a microphone
   in a basement off 14th
    street balancing
   the world on his fingers like a balloon

or the little black bat
 who sees by the light of the song
   she carries between her teeth

has mosquitoes enough to eat & doesn't need to own
      the land?

A SINGLE LIVEOAK BRANCH, SECRET PATH

cities of dust. badland cities
dusted with parapets of snow. how I
look, making it all human

under the snaking oak-bark
waterdusty lichen congregates along a flow
flowers & continents

white & green, mysterious glyphic signs almost
letters I make up to make up for my
lack of learning,

one waterdrop reflecting sky & underworld.
dank black ledges up above
rich moss, star-tendrill'd, hanging on

the shape I want to have in the air
the mistake that I was meant to
control the planet,

one pale scimitar'd spider
earthquakes & floods, a single
feathered lonely seed of chaparral broom

a ring around the sun
the water full of ice needles
trying to breathe all day.

in & out Frenchmans Canyon
where the wagon road's choked
with old snow
burroweed & young pinyon

let me walk on the path more consciously
from now on,
let fear not drive me from consciousness

BRIDGEPORT, CALIFORNIA

buncha deer & bobcats

sittin around in the Trails Restaurant

chewin the fat

human heads on the wall

NORTH COUNTRY

we been making these bargains so long
it's a goddam conspiracy when the sun rises
smoke & platinum
somebody's fat white dog gettin ready to
knock over the amanita muscaria again

up here you could spend all night draggin your
unborn children down the roads of the pygmy forest
until you try to make a fire with your teeth.
no use your silver bullets,
no use the funny crystals that you borrowed from the ocean.

these are the rules & there are no regrets. up here
they string their guitars with rattlesnake grass
& their violins with the feathers of an eagle.
the tombstones on the hill were all
handcrafted by jealous husbands.

III

The City

THE DANCE

                    when you
throw your leg up on me
it rocks
              back and outward
you can get dragged under & there are savage
fishes

GULHANE HOTEL POEM

1. In Istanbul in the Gulhane Hotel wake up
and pick off crab lice
around the balls

in the valleys of Anatolia
in the white morning
in the world

this is made
this is done
in a cavern of the flesh

the janitor leaned his
broom against the brown
door
and laughing so
and flickering, left.
they have prior knowledge

I tore the sweater off a German junkie. what is
accomplished by that.

and they gather
by the stove, it is their brotherhood
on opium, inattentive
Indian
faces, German mouths
the fire is like a
tree and they touch it like
animals.
they are allowed to say nothing about
time.

upstairs in a raid they
took the blond
boy out of the movies
"this trip they don't come back"

2. I am burnt
to a hand
the bones of
a face in your
memory,
I exist in Gulhane Hotel
behind the comfortable
front doors of your smile
where you sleep
with Doug in Pennsylvania
white room full of rain

the hand that is my face now
bites my
lips and moustache
bright like grass in the dream
and they will bring hashish many
times and break it in
the pipe. and I will take the
red ember high into my brain
circle of faces
watching. and you are almost a photograph

3. Damascus
            hash rolled in covered street, old town
closed shops, dusty corrugated tin, look out
for soldiers
then old men
follow us
in thru alleys, scream welcomes again to
Frankish disguised
foreigners

large gold hair, we wind
blown in dark cloaks, bearded
arriving

Paul rolls
joint first burning hash in tinfoil

the Street that is called Straight

clawed silver hands, enormous cock, cloudless room

children wait for baksheesh with
mouths turned down
sick on all of it, falafel, arabic, white mosque, smiling
                              winding but it's no good
get tea for 20 piastres and wander in gray
smoke.

Marie with us. Paul said, stupid
"I could ball that girl"
I saw her later
lying on dark beach with her only child.

we left Syria
blue houses were warning the Angel of Death

THE ADVENTURES OF THE FLOATING RABBI
(a novel in eight chapters)

chapter one
the kindly mescaline chateau

an evening in the mescaline chateau, no
lamps, no bulbs, just clean twilight from
outside fingering thru windows. amphibian
shapes of the servants. you were told they
were colored people. they don't approve of
taking mescaline. and you say oh no . . .
weariness of a fallen empire. you have
forgotten the ambiguous splendors of new
york and san francisco. dying you have
forgotten this is a dream.

chapter two
loosing the venomous arthropods

quite near the chateau, everyone was ready
in the quiet hillside town. the peasants
turned out with banners and the rich tourists
with cameras. weren't they surprised when
someone let the giant spiders loose. wow
watch them go.

chapter three
many deaths and reappearances

thru the agonies of the spiders he taught
us death was a dream. he gave me antidotes
when I lapsed unconscious. otherwise bat-
tering the brutes with sticks — tarantula
forepaws crushed, crab carapaces leaking
green and violet juice. always wake up &
run some more. on a quiet dirt hillside
he preached to us the resurrection of the
meat. then they took him away and his
secret antidote too.

41

chapter four
underwater near hiroshima

now you're in the jungle on your own. faces
of asian and australian soldiers lifting
carefully their rifles always get you.
underwater in the coral reefs off hiro-
shima you keep coming. many white animals
gliding like bones in the mist. shark and
barracuda. where else can you go now.

chapter five
fred the schizophrenic

back in the chateau we had to cope with a
secret schizophrenic. posed an ambiguous
threat, definitely murderous but gentle
as a lamb and no one believed us when we
explained that he had to be executed.
outside the night was flecked with scram-
bled eggs. he left a yellow trail wherever
he went in his insane pursuit of the virgin.
when we returned from the store he had been
eliminated.

chapter six
breakfast under the mountain

northward we sailed thru the ice river. I
couldn't remember which side was greenland.
old stone barns under a mountain. ate break-
fast in a viking cathedral and had to change
money explaining to the unseen lady at my
side all the places I had been. later the
tourists took a moral dislike to the na-

tionality of our guides and split for the
southland. more room for us — shimmering
empty water.

chapter seven
a ski race to your draft board

it ended on a snowy mountain. futile to
recount the immense journeys which brought
us here. we skiied downward in the fluid
darkness thru thick trees. the last pitch
was an empty hospital waitingroom, tilting
downward and unlit. a cameraman posed all
the racers as they came. afraid of his line
of talk I said fuck it and descended while
he was unprepared. sailing on thru the far
door it turned out to be the draft board.
appointments for the shrink, to save my ass
once again, I took a seat between my dad
and the hashish scarab.

chapter eight

his breath was twin
buffaloes trudging down the
map of the pacific slope he used
to carry in his eyes. never going
to remember the burning
desolation freeway, a mask
full of butterflies
might have been his
hands so softly
wailing
nothing that we have
built will make the
sun rise again
he sings
a penniless song
& jogs on down thru
fireweed & black sage. the
faces of his children dwindled to white
pebbles
as many of them among the
fireflies and stars.

CAT POME

cats are wise not in space
        but in time
        I see that as under the
        moonlight & I dance my gray
good cat
        & go in the shadow under
 luminous trees
 & inside by a moon
enormous granite wall my child Lorie
  learns to behave to its rhythm praying in her
  sleep, premenstrual
        monthly fever 102
            today in her ass
& I saw that the cat looked on
        many universes
        thru the same grainy eye
he delights to lead you from one
        to one
        if you run blindly thru the
        earth
a nail goes thru yr ears each step
  & the cat is lisping clearly
        of reimannian dimensions
a gray neural space infinitely
  far beyond the voices
the cat says it's a dream radio
that photographs yr woman crying
because she hates death. far away

in a bright room with yellow &
red curtains, burlap, rain
on the wall & death falls
    freely all night
was in the street below
    again & again in
her dreams the cop is
death & nobody knows

the rain is really on the wall

& the moon-goddess is no joke

    as she answers to the name you
    give her across the pillow

:there are mysterious gray spaces in the

    shining

should I go into the high mtns. & fast crosslegged
on talus in the blizzard? there black
rock wings cross above the air
& ask me questions I don't understand

there the animal might die in hair-colored stone

blindly thru the earth, wise
as an old man who never learned to talk

    I'm shaking in my chest, strong
      fingers
    have a rhythm & they don't
      understand pain now
after my circus in the moonlight

paranoid, narks
saw me dancing with the cat?

yesterday I fastened my organs to the screen
  1968 election
       fools the eye
          entrails hanging in time,

    today I dance to the women of the moon

who love me
        and everyday

I move with you, yr tide

has pomes I dance against

   them in a Jewish language

whose aphorisms contrast with the silence
    cats maintain
        in their wisdom

   as the moon

    and the wind of
     god that quickens the dry bones

oh yes I am going to go sit on iron mtn. until the skin wears
off from my grave & I can
start asking some real questions
& talk to the stars without interpreters

KATA

platinum glints off sun oil
surface of water in the yard now

the last cherry blossoms
wept in an industrial storm

this morning driving to work practiced
backhand striking to collarbone

or bridge of nose stalled at red light.
at war I am practicing

the water rising green over stone
into complete darkness

not a wind to move the candles
flame under the rain

walk over the water shining
flat now with my ghosts

in the yard under the
center of my belly crying

IYOI

at peace with the circles
of water and shells of me

drop off into infinite
light and darkness

so many faces the repetitions wear me
"could I interest you in a book of my own poetry"
blurring the impulse, I can't remember,
the Avenue, strangers
wake them up out of first genial greeting
me over coffee & burned dead meat.
stoned or drunk
or piercing me suddenly with verbal energy
"trading the dinosaur bones of our ancestors"
my head bent sideways beyond the potted
plants to look out for the persian
proprietor——threatened to break my
fingers in the D——
disturbing the mellow
atmosphere of changing money

no solid ground: a surface developed
between me & the planet,
jesus freaks talk about hell,
my spirit
given out half-open to so many
almost like a rock star.
concrete & junkies,
a small crinkle of dollars in my pocket.

BENDING DOWN TOGETHER TO THE ELECTRIC GUITAR
we had to split. joel heard me say you should KNOW
RIGHT ON THIRD WORLD BROTHER
i smacked him soft with an elbow in the
gut
in the wilderness rock
an roll stoned purple lite
a diversion for the gentiles
bleak headlite machine up ashby
john
in the context of that
touch
WHAT

WHAT WHAT
black rumbling heart dog

what what what whats the
matter motherfucker a muffler in the road

LIVING IN THE BONEYARD

lime condensed on the ceiling, or maybe
    yellow
        spider eggs
           X in yellow chalk where pete tried to
                mark the rain,
           last winter

        but it gets in anyway
                got to use inkrags to soak it
                up

           this is living in the boneyard.
a golden lion of Judah
        grins out of the menorah
           I never lit this year.
        next to my elbow the sea is
           full of dying birds
        suck up their curses & breathe on me
                again boys, it's
           a long way to the end of the world but if
                you let your breath out slowly in the
           middle of the first
              line maybe no one
will notice

DISTANCES

a lion cradles close to my chest
sucking her bottle
stares on within.

historical view, fragments of the lower horizon
a seal carved of jade, pieces of alloy wire, wool
tufts maybe, poems illegible, charcoal burned beams
serpentine intrusion, open to the sky
my bones and the bones of my daughter.

MAYA

last year's tan oak leaves, dust, down of black chickens,
                                        shitting
I find I am attached to the earth by ten thousand
things. one child minds the wood stove — the other
turns the flashlight upside
down and says "no no baby" — the land has been sold,
we're here like hungry trespassers, keeping
up a small existence.

this black guy comes out of my backyard at 1 AM
swinging a blue crowbar.
I'm shuffling naked out the door to confront him
"you there" he says to me
"you look like a David
but why do you wear your hair so long
what do you see
you standing there without your clothes better
watch it when it's a carload of
cops and J. Edgar Hoover and all their numbers"
and he's gone away up the block,
not till morning did I understand

under the colored ramadan lights
   my lady of the night
   sings poems counterpoint
   the burning of my hair
   and stifled tongue
   thru redblack glass
   a splintering of gold
   her lit cigarette caresses my balls
   in the back saloon of the arab cafe

the limbs of my animal
   movement bound
   to a brass bedframe,
   roped to the chandeliers
   i've dreamed
   so long to be the victim
   and the sacred child,
   my dream the lady
   moves about me gently
   torturing.
   enacted thru a glass
   i scream and come.

when i was a man
   i gave up childish things
   gave up jacking off
   for nearly a month
   after my 12th birthday

when I see you I always want to say

you look like my brother

or a friend I used to know

why don't you come over and . . .

I could love you if I ever could love any man

you standing there in the mirror

looking so pretty & so woe-begone

PICTURE OF A RED BULL STRIDING
ON ITS HIND LEGS INTO FOREST
BEARING AN EMPTY FIELD OF WORDS

ah well
            elbows grinding carbon table
            torsion and a crowd of
                    numbers slipping thru the
            hole in my sleeve
                rubbing fingers up thru
                        eye sockets to
                demonstrate to sophisticated
                inhabitants of cloudbound worlds
                    the existence of stars.
            ten billion years went by.
        who could I explain to?
            "in those days we
            lived on a planet in small wooden
                        rooms"
        who would listen.

rain on yellow dozers & tangled eucalyptus debris
rain in small waves on mudshiny trail
rain on edges of my gray hat
rain on red volcanic shield disclosed between pine-duff
rain on monterey pine's lit sexual candles
rain on snake's flames indian paintbrush
rain on yarrow
rain on coyote brush
earth drinking the rain, carrying poison oxides
to earth, smog washed away
rain on young grasses shivering
rain on poison oak shining with new leaves
rain on sound of the wind
rain on the faint poem-page
rain on the pocket mouse's 6 small molars,
she will need them no more,
they gleam in humped shining of skunk-shit
rain sphered & glowing on the sharp needles of pine
rain on my boots reflecting the sky's face
rain on Bluejay's scribbled sentences

sun-face sad eyes sweat beads
down your grass cheeks.

you showed me the map
of the counties of California,
river to river
impenetrable names & color

call from the far end of the thicket
tell me to hurry,

the danger I will get involved in chewing out the lumberjacks
"all the same to me buddy sacred grove"

BORDER

on the paper is a thin black line
one side, contour mountains & valleys
blue reservoirs & dead yellow for urban

other side without features, plain yellow.

a cyclone fence & concertina wire, one side
people living in cardboard
boxes on the floodplain
                      other side little league, trailbikes
                      San Diego! no way
                      to write about it.
           I'm a tourist here amid dreams & TV shows
                  only,
an animal without a ground
    coyote running on wet 8 freeway

you can cross the fence into Mexico, no one
        asks questions, a man waves only
        leaflets at us which we shrug away.

how poor they are! we exclaim.

Rio Guadelupe, mesas, willows, baby
repeating something audible in another language
        across the river, reeds
& stagnant water lurking brilliant with skyblue

it was a day of broken clouds & sunlight
Ensenada, we are princes of Norteamericano spending dollars
hand-weave of copper birds,
doves under the cross-pole
candlepole to heaven
embroidered amanita
    and leather of red flowers

we have come in to spend,
the depression makes everyone so hungry
no tiene pollo,

one side of the thin line.
            a border

is a mechanism of economics

to keep the dollars on one side
& the many children's mouths
        on the other.

Garrett Hardin ecologist says the cyclone
fence is one wall
            of a life
                boat.
he says that food
should not be thrown to the people
starving in the
blank featureless
                sea

other lines are drawn closer
to home: concentric
    survival maps,

        dollars spent on
the other side of the border skateboards & heroin
the barrio is full the suburb is empty
the parkinglot is full the shopping center is empty
the Third Avenue News is full of men looking at priceless
sexual treasures: a man in a color photograph
hooked to a wall of wood,
fastened in leather,
a black woman carefully burning his underarm hair
with a kitchen match

up here they say "aliens"
        24-hour plane & truck patrol
"looking for a man broke into the cabins of Jacumba
            an alien"
"lookin for a mexican or a canadian or whatever
            with a gun"

up here they lost their children
still are looking for them
            picked up on a 502
            last seen skidding at 60
            on a 90 dollar a day habit
but you aren't supposed to let on
that they mentioned it to anyone,

your brother will betray you

they say "aliens"
down near Ensenada they say "banditos"
dragged the honeymoon kids out of
their camper in the moonlight
stuck their switchblades in him
            why not, they have nothing
                de nada.

which side of the border
did you ask to be born on?

will you send your melted
ice cream cones to the children
of Ensenada?

does a cyclone fence hold water?

    for the answer to these and other questions
"state your citizenship and what articles
you acquired outside the United States"

"I'm an American we all are
we bought about 45 dollars worth
of curios in Ensenada"

HOSPITAL: MERCY SAN JUAN

Chicano boy pulls out the grass that there should be
nothing alive on the way to the mercy place,

a death room,
abstract cross

a priest speaks across the grave
One Life to Live on the TV

we carry feathers & carnations into this atmosphere,
Bernice stares into the void wind

tells us not to worry.
the sunlight grinds & fades on iron

balconies, stone terraces, a mirror
series of rooms

we imagine dead people waking up in here,
becoming children again,

putting on new lives like a suit of used
clothes from goodwill —

on the metal cross
Jesus imagines he is forsaken,

Jan kicks her legs nervously
Bernice turns from her child

into the great expanse.
we speak of Sumerians and flying saucers.

everything shaking out of the way it ought to be
                    when the storm signals are up
          I got no patience, can't you see?
                    tell you and tell you
                    need a road
no way to retreat
                    so sorry
all morning at the supermarket
                    worrying me like a dog after a bone
                    what you want?
let go, need space this morning
                    love you but so tired
                    the clown face
                    natural fool the village idiot
                    fellow in the mirror go these
                    bags around his eyes
                              can't tell
you screaming over tea
inside the broken
house the fuchsias
                    way it ought to be

QUEEN OF WANDS

you sit all by yourself in that blue
canyon of yours on top of the world
"baby cat, baby cat" & you clutch her to your breast
but all your lions are made of stone
& there is no happiness in this
world for a clear-eyed woman.
Things are flowering,
the sun is a huge daisy
your mind can see beyond the purple mountains
but everywhere it's the same old story
& all your cat cares about anyway is her
dinner & secret psychic relationships
with the powers of the night

THE HANGED MAN

the man who is tied to a tree

whose eyes are perfectly empty
of everything but himself & his own projections

who drowns himself in fire
like a lizard

downward, suspended
          by the circling of the world
                    from a live oak

who defies the thermodynamics of possibility

who eats his own fantasy
who can't remember

the man who is grown into a tree
his bark is smooth as the madrone

the man who sets a fire
in his own skull
for a jewel of perception

hanging perfectly
          relaxed by his toes like a
                    buzzard in the middle of space

who sees the past & future at once
& immediately forgets them

POEM BEGINNING WITH A LINE BY SUNTREE

"children rub antlers"
>fuzzy
>hand to her mouth, trying to
>>remember her dream
>>but the name went away
>with the part that was scary
>& the houses like tiny
people opening their
>mouths
>>a deer in the back of her mind
>>that she never has seen
>>>saying her
>>secret
>name
>over & over
wake up
>>wake up

DRY SPELL

Go crázy skinning my brain for poems
spoon out the bowl, there must be one more
drop in there,
flavored of cinnamon, how sweet
sweat, musk, tags of human feeling, birth & death
now everyone can taste it
thin skull rind.

WARNING

beware of the man with moon in cancer
eyes of jade & a bronze beard

he will trade you a poem
for a kiss of abalone

he will trade you the one-eyed moon
for a taste of what you've seen

he will move thru your bed preoccupied
with his love of himself

till you're sponging your heart from the floor
where you spilled the wine

ON THE RIDGE

people go around dressed up like tarot cards
the hawk-nosed clown,
the tooth mother with a lot to say
the emperor cross-legged among his mountains
the born loser who pays up turquoise with a smile,
get trapped behind the faces?
what does it do for me
to be who my friends think I am?
years break the mask & I
pick up the pieces to make another one.
how does it taste on your tongue,
the blindfolded woman with two swords,
the preacher with a crown of hawk feathers.

CALIFORNIA STREET

sourgrass
trailing thru the rear wheel
of an abandoned bike,
spider's paradise
& bluejay cries,
I overhear the neighbors
& pass judgments.

SPIRAL

kitchen match struck from sandstone of a half-glazed mug
the most impossible detail
spiral of bighorn sheep's one horn, the right
yerba santa, golden seal, cannabis & peppermint
beautiful lines of gas-heat convected thru atmosphere
how can I do without run-on lines, the sentences are endless.
equally empty, trying to decide
the phonecalls with money
hummocks of boulders on the moon
procrastination, envelopes unlicked in piles
clay dog in peyote sand with a closed mouth
water dribbling
stoned, spiralled, crystalled, vortexed
golden seal & honey, a spoon
a horn reflecting
I have been keeper of game paths for the city
making the world again
flashing thru crystal
work for which no one will pay
squawking, flex on air, queer cry of flicker from pines
the sun moving already
quick turn of lip to lip after all we forgot
the center of the horn's spiral in mudgrass beyond the horn
the crater hidden, boulders concentric
how could I confess, not here
the eye dropped from the eye
the mouth dropped from the telephone
texture of territorial damage
elegant detail
waste of gas & waste of whale meat
waste of sulfur
waste of glazed clay
stomping on a straw mat made of fog to make the world
leaf on shadow
crystal
failed communication

money disappears inside a mouth
the movement of light at 20 billion years
the Lady stamping her foot impatient
mind on a string like dog held tuned & quivering
Coyote and Bighorn and Jesus and Bluejay and Jehovah
let's see,
look,
leaf-pattern on the brown fur, golden, detail of
scent of deer & flicker, huge ghosts
I swallowed the roach like a sacrifice
elegant lines on the horn
impact of words against the table vibrating
concentric boulders outward thrown from Aristarchus
shadow
monkey flower, golden seal, artemisia
the map I made with money & death in certain corners
spinning in front of my face
a tuft of cotton on the green god
language
charms & flavors of the smallest bits of
shadow & revelation
green grass again in winterspring
earth's movement
tickling her underleaf
what I want to do
lose the track, find again
turn the horn, ribbed
fleas under the beautiful fur,
square lines on the map
a world without memory
the evolution of the earth and the moon
tetrahydracannabinol
the open mouth of the sea
the mouth of the horn
my fingers in the brush by my mouth
whispering, lingering
tongue-kiss, tooth-kiss, kiss of herbs

groin-kiss, kiss of smoke
incompetence with the typewriter
in which a universe can be made but not included
sweetness & mint
the letter in the back house, 2 years of dust on it
pathways
the match burnt out on the table like a black bud
never finished, only abandoned
a woman's mouth outside the poem
a pair of legs across the street, two eyes
the endless sentence
groin in the crater's shadow
neural lingerings of fire by my hand
the vice of procrastination, postponement, the sin
blue air
blue earth
sunflowers withered, shadow of Copernicus
the darkness of the mouth
no other planet
an ocean of air
tingling
never
last edge of light on brush of the dog's fur

I came down to the stones of the bay
the moon was on the other side
there was no one around but the moon.
I was walking in the mudflats.
Old tires stuck to my toes.
The face of the moon was made of all the poems
I could possibly write in all my possible lifetimes.
Seagulls were eating my poems.
Mirror images of words floated on the water.
The poems were made of ice, fog & bones.
I stuck them to my skin & made them into wings
the color of coral & styrofoam.
Just then people started streaming thru to the
free pizza just beyond the shooting gallery
I was flying over their heads,
dragging tires, dripping mud in their faces.
I came down to the shores of the bay.
"What have you done with my poems?" I asked the moon.

Produced at The Print Center, Inc., Box 1050, Brooklyn, N.Y., 11202, a non-profit printing facility for literary and arts-related publications. Funded by The New York State Council on the Arts and the National Endowment for the Arts.

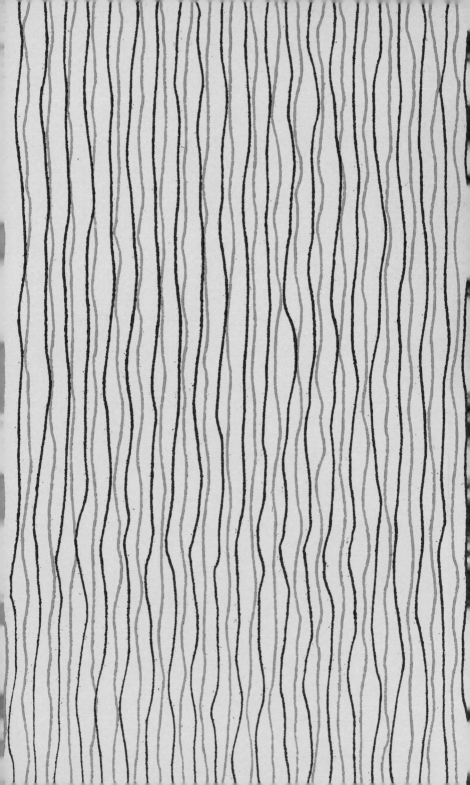